THIRD GRADE WORKBOOKS:
English is Fun

SPEEDY PUBLISHING LLC

Speedy Publishing LLC
40 E. Main St. #1156
Newark, DE 19711
www.speedypublishing.com

Copyright 2015

ISBN: 978-1-6814-5481-8

First Printed 03/24/2015

All Rights reserved. No part of this book may be reproduced or used in any way or form or by any means whether electronic or mechanical, this means that you cannot record or photocopy any material ideas or tips that are provided in this book

Plural Forms

Write in the blank space provided the plural form of the words on the left.

1. abyss _____

2. alumnus _____

3. analysis _____

4. aquarium _____

5. arch _____

6. atlas _____

7. axe _____

8. baby _____

9. bacterium _____

10. batch _____

11. beach _____

12. brush   _____

13. bus   _____

14. calf   _____

15. chateau   _____

16. cherry   _____

17. child   _____

18. church   _____

19. circus _____

20. city _____

21. cod _____

22. copy _____

23. crisis _____

24. curriculum _____

25. deer _____

26. dictionary   _____

27. domino   _____

28. dwarf   _____

29. echo   _____

30. elf   _____

31. emphasis   _____

32. family   _____

33. fax _____

34. fish _____

35. flush _____

36. fly _____

37. foot _____

38. fungus _____

39. half _____

40. hero   _____

41. hippopotamus _____

42. hoax   _____

43. hoof   _____

44. index   _____

45. iris   _____

46. kiss   _____

47. knife _____

48. lady   _____

49. leaf   _____

50. life   _____

51. loaf   _____

52. man   _____

53. mango _____

54. memorandum _____

55. mess _____

56. moose _____

57. motto _____

58. mouse _____

59. nanny _____

60. neurosis _____

61. nucleus _____

62. oasis _____

63. octopus _____

64. party _____

65. pass _____

66. penny _____

67. person _____

68. plateau _____

69. poppy _____

70. potato _____

71. quiz _____

72. reflex _____

73. runner-up _____

74. scarf _____

75. scratch _____

76. series _____

77. sheaf _____

78. sheep _____

79. shelf _____

80. son-in-law _____

81. species _____

82. splash   _____

83. spy   _____

84. stitch   _____

85. story   _____

86. syllabus   _____

87. tax   _____

88. thesis   _____

89. thief _____

90. tomato _____

91. tooth _____

92. tornado _____

93. try _____

94. volcano _____

95. waltz _____

96. wash _____

97. watch _____

98. wharf _____

99. wife _____

100. woman _____

Nouns

Identify whether the word is a noun or not. Write YES if the word is a noun and NO if not.

1. age　　　　　　　　　　　_____

2. walking　　　　　　　　　_____

3. February　　　　　　　　_____

4. talk　　　　　　　　　　_____

5. John _____

6. hold _____

7. April _____

8. beautiful _____

9. bird _____

10. bounced _____

11. attractive _____

12. Helen   _____

13. worked   _____

14. captain   _____

15. sneeze   _____

16. artist   _____

17. charming   _____

18. sculptor   _____

19. typed   _____

20. ball   _____

21. car   _____

22. quit   _____

23. Tuesday   _____

24. big   _____

25. January   _____

Verbs
(Past, Present, Future Tenses)

SCORE
_____

Identify if the verb is <u>Past</u>, <u>Present</u> or <u>Future</u> Tense)

1. sing _____

2. yell _____

3. accelerated _____

4. wanted   _____

5. will walk   _____

6. will jog   _____

7. itches   _____

8. pushes   _____

9. will call   _____

10. will own   _____

11. ended   _____

12. met   _____

13. gave   _____

14. flew   _____

15. reads   _____

16. pulls   _____

17. going to play _____

18. will clean _____

19. noted _____

20. pinned _____

21. write _____

22. lay _____

23. will make _____

24. will do _____

25. crashes   _____

26. sat   _____

27. took   _____

28. will be   _____

29. wrote   _____

30. laughed   _____

31. will examine   _____

32. sells   _____

33. finished   _____

34. will practice _____

35. will have   _____

36. had   _____

37. did   _____

38. do   _____

39. draw _____

40. noticed _____

41. paid _____

42. will perform _____

43. will do _____

44. matches _____

45. leaps _____

46. will lick   _____

47. locked   _____

48. injure   _____

49. influenced   _____

50. includes   _____

Adjectives

SCORE
_____

Identify whether the word is an adjective or not. Write YES if the word is an adjective and NO if not.

1. cute   _____

2. hunt   _____

3. gather   _____

4. fine   _____

5. House   _____

6. colorful   _____

7. jolly   _____

8. Wednesday   _____

9. delightful   _____

10. television   _____

11. handsome   _____

12. clever _____

13. formulate _____

14. arrogant _____

15. November _____

16. sleepy _____

17. Dad _____

18. energetic _____

19. computer　　　　　＿＿＿＿＿＿＿

20. brainy　　　　　　＿＿＿＿＿＿＿

21. keep　　　　　　　＿＿＿＿＿＿＿

22. easy　　　　　　　＿＿＿＿＿＿＿

23. Ms. Smith　　　　＿＿＿＿＿＿＿

24. hug　　　　　　　＿＿＿＿＿＿＿

25. adorable　　　　　＿＿＿＿＿＿＿

SCORE
_____

Pronouns

Identify whether the word is a pronoun or not. Write YES if the word is a pronoun and NO if not.

1. I _____

2. jag _____

3. you _____

4. tiles _____

5. he _____

6. wood _____

7. she _____

8. shows _____

9. it _____

10. judged _____

11. they _____

12. forecast _____

13. we _____

14. led _____

15. me _____

16. gray _____

17. him _____

18. red _____

19. her   _____

20. stones   _____

21. us   _____

22. beach   _____

23. them   _____

24. trees   _____

25. yourself   _____

Adverbs

Identify whether the adverb is a <u>How</u>, <u>When</u>, <u>Where</u> or <u>To What Extent</u> Adverb,

1. eagerly   _____

2. carefully   _____

3. sloppily   _____

4. after   _____

5. before   _____

6. now   _____

7. everywhere   _____

8. somewhere   _____

9. outside   _____

10. very   _____

11. too   _____

12. extremely _____

13. really _____

14. quite _____

15. upstairs _____

16. there _____

17. soon _____

18. annually _____

19. loyally _____

20. grimly _____

21. briskly _____

22. quickly _____

23. inside _____

24. when _____

25. rather _____

Answers

Plural Forms

Write in the blank space provided the plural form of the words on the left.

1. abyss — abysses
2. alumnus — alumni
3. analysis — analyses
4. aquarium — aquaria
5. arch — arches
6. atlas — atlases
7. axe — axes
8. baby — babies
9. bacterium — bacteria
10. batch — batches
11. beach — beaches
12. brush — brushes
13. bus — buses
14. calf — calves
15. chateau — chateaux
16. cherry — cherries
17. child — children
18. church — churches
19. circus — circuses
20. city — cities

21.	cod	cod
22.	copy	copies
23.	crisis	crises
24.	curriculum	curricula
25.	deer	deer
26.	dictionary	dictionaries
27.	domino	dominoes
28.	dwarf	dwarves
29.	echo	echoes
30.	elf	elves
31.	emphasis	emphases
32.	family	families
33.	fax	faxes
34.	fish	fish
35.	flush	flushes
36.	fly	flies
37.	foot	feet
38.	fungus	fungi
39.	half	halves
40.	hero	heroes
41.	hippopotamus	hippopotami
42.	hoax	hoaxes
43.	hoof	hooves
44.	index	indexes
45.	iris	irises
46.	kiss	kisses
47.	knife	knives
48.	lady	ladies
49.	leaf	leaves
50.	life	lives
51.	loaf	loaves
52.	man	men
53.	mango	mangoes
54.	memorandum	memoranda
55.	mess	messes
56.	moose	moose
57.	motto	mottoes
58.	mouse	mice
59.	nanny	nannies

60.	neurosis	neuroses
61.	nucleus	nuclei
62.	oasis	oases
63.	octopus	octopi
64.	party	parties
65.	pass	passes
66.	penny	pennies
67.	person	people
68.	plateau	plateaux
69.	poppy	poppies
70.	potato	potatoes
71.	quiz	quizzes
72.	reflex	reflexes
73.	runner-up	runners-up
74.	scarf	scarves
75.	scratch	scratches
76.	series	series
77.	sheaf	sheaves
78.	sheep	sheep
79.	shelf	shelves
80.	son-in-law	sons-in-laws
81.	pecies	species
82.	splash	splashes
83.	spy	spies
84.	stitch	stitches
85.	story	stories
86.	syllabus	syllabi
87.	tax	taxes
88.	thesis	theses
89.	thief	thieves
90.	tomato	tomatoes
91.	tooth	teeth
92.	tornado	tornadoes
93.	try	tries
94.	volcano	volcanoes
95.	waltz	waltzes
96.	wash	washes
97.	watch	watches
98.	wharf	wharves

99. wife   wives
100. woman   women

Nouns

Identify whether the word is a noun or not. Write YES if the word is a noun and NO if not.

1. age — YES
2. walking — NO
3. February — YES
4. talk — NO
5. John — YES
6. hold — NO
7. April — YES
8. beautiful — NO
9. bird — YES
10. bounced — NO
11. attractive — NO
12. Helen — YES
13. worked — NO
14. captain — YES
15. sneeze — NO
16. artist — YES
17. charming — NO
18. sculptor — YES
19. typed — NO
20. ball — YES
21. car — YES
22. quit — NO
23. Tuesday — YES
24. big — NO
25. January — YES

Verbs (Past, Present, Future Tenses)

Identify if the verb is <u>Past</u>, <u>Present</u> or <u>Future</u> Tense)

1.	sing	Present
2.	yell	Present
3.	accelerated	Past
4.	wanted	Past
5.	will walk	Future
6.	will jog	Future
7.	itches	Present
8.	pushes	Present
9.	will call	Future
10.	will own	Future
11.	ended	Past
12.	met	Past
13.	gave	Past
14.	flew	Past
15.	reads	Present
16.	pulls	Present
17.	going to play	Future
18.	will clean	Future
19.	noted	Past
20.	pinned	Past
21.	write	Present
22.	lay	Present
23.	will make	Future
24.	will do	Future
25.	crashes	Present
26.	sat	Past
27.	took	Past
28.	will be	Future
29.	wrote	Past
30.	laughed	Past
31.	will examine	Future
32.	sells	Present
33.	finished	Past
34.	will practice	Future

35.	will have	Future
36.	had	Past
37.	did	Past
38.	do	Present
39.	draw	Present
40.	noticed	Past
41.	paid	Past
42.	will perform	Future
43.	will do	Future
44.	matches	Present
45.	leaps	Present
46.	will lick	Future
47.	locked	Past
48.	injure	Present
49.	influenced	Past
50.	includes	Present

Adjectives

Identify whether the word is an adjective or not. Write YES if the word is an adjective and NO if not.

1.	cute	YES
2.	hunt	NO
3.	gather	NO
4.	fine	YES
5.	House	NO
6.	colorful	YES
7.	jolly	YES
8.	Wednesday	NO
9.	delightful	YES
10.	television	NO
11.	handsome	YES
12.	clever	YES
13.	formulate	NO
14.	arrogant	YES
15.	November	NO
16.	sleepy	YES

17.	Dad	NO
18.	energetic	YES
19.	computer	NO
20.	brainy	YES
21.	keep	NO
22.	easy	YES
23.	Ms. Smith	NO
24.	hug	NO
25.	adorable	YES

Pronouns

Identify whether the word is a pronoun or not. Write YES if the word is a pronoun and NO if not.

1.	I	YES
2.	jag	NO
3.	you	YES
4.	tiles	NO
5.	he	YES
6.	wood	NO
7.	she	YES
8.	shows	NO
9.	it	YES
10.	judged	NO
11.	they	YES
12.	forecast	NO
13.	we	YES
14.	led	NO
15.	me	YES
16.	gray	NO
17.	him	YES
18.	red	NO
19.	her	YES
20.	stones	NO
21.	us	YES
22.	beach	NO
23.	them	YES

24. trees — NO
25. yourself — YES

Adverbs

Identify whether the adverb is a <u>How</u>, <u>When</u>, <u>Where</u> or <u>To What Extent</u> Adverb.

1. eagerly — HOW
2. carefully — HOW
3. sloppily — HOW
4. after — WHEN
5. before — WHEN
6. now — WHEN
7. everywhere — WHERE
8. somewhere — WHERE
9. outside — WHERE
10. very — TO WHAT EXTENT
11. too — TO WHAT EXTENT
12. extremely — TO WHAT EXTENT
13. really — TO WHAT EXTENT
14. quite — TO WHAT EXTENT
15. upstairs — WHERE
16. there — WHERE
17. soon — WHEN
18. annually — WHEN
19. loyally — HOW
20. grimly — HOW
21. briskly — HOW
22. quickly — HOW
23. inside — WHERE
24. when — WHEN
25. rather — TO WHAT EXTENT

Lightning Source UK Ltd.
Milton Keynes UK
UKHW052048110820
368081UK00007B/48